Madam C.J. Walker
and the Her Beauty Empire

Caitie McAneney

PowerKiDS press.

New York

Published in 2017 by The Rosen Publishing Group, Inc.
29 East 21st Street, New York, NY 10010

First Edition

Editor: Sarah Machajewski
Book Design: Mickey Harmon

Photo Credits: Cover, pp. 1–10, 12–14, 16–32 (series design) Melodist/Shutterstock.com; cover, p. 5 (Madam C. J. Walker) Michael Ochs Archives/Stringer/ Michael Ochs Archives/Getty Images; p. 7 Print Collector/Contributor/Hulton Archive/Getty Images; p. 8 https://en.wikipedia.org/wiki/File:A%27Lelia_Walker.jpg; p. 9 Interim Archives/Contributor/Archive Photos/Getty Images; pp. 11, 21 courtesy of the Library of Congress; p. 13 https://en.wikipedia.org/wiki/File:Annie_Malone.jpg; p. 15 Everett Historical/Shutterstock.com; p. 16 dawncollector/Flickr.com; p. 17 Evan Finch/Flickr.com; p. 19 (inset) https://commons.wikimedia.org/w/index.php?title=File:Madam_CJ_Walker_Manufacturing_Company,_Indianapolis,_Indiana(1911).jpg&oldid=163277176; pp. 19, 23, 27 Afro Newspaper/Gado/Archive Photos/Getty Images; p. 25 https://commons.wikimedia.org/wiki/File:Villa-lewaro_crop.jpg; p. 26 https://commons.wikimedia.org/wiki/File:MadameCJWalkerdrivingautomoblie.png; p. 29 Raymond Boyd/Contributor/Michael Ochs Archives.

Cataloging-in-Publication Data

Names: McAneney, Caitie.
Title: Madam C.J. Walker and her beauty empire / Caitie McAneney.
Description: New York : PowerKids Press, 2017. | Series: Great entrepreneurs in U.S. history | Includes index.
Identifiers: ISBN 9781499421316 (pbk.) | ISBN 9781499421330 (library bound) | ISBN 9781499421323 (6 pack)
Subjects: LCSH: Walker, C. J., Madam, 1867-1919–Juvenile literature. | African American women executives–Biography–Juvenile literature. | Cosmetics industry–United States–History–Juvenile literature.
Classification: LCC HD9970.5.C672 M34 2017 | DDC 338.7'66855'092–d23

Manufactured in the United States of America

CPSIA Compliance Information: Batch #BS16PK: For Further Information contact Rosen Publishing, New York, New York at 1-800-237-9932

Contents

Self-Made Millionare

Madam C. J. Walker's life had a simple beginning. However, in the 51 years that she lived, she became one of the most extraordinary entrepreneurs of her time. She was born into a family of former slaves, and she lived among the violence and injustice of the post-Civil War South. Out of her hardships, she found inspiration to build a greater life for herself and her daughter.

Today, many consider Madam C. J. Walker to be the first female African American millionaire. Her business was based on providing effective hair-care products for African American women, but it offered more than that. Walker's products also held the promise of **refinement** and confidence. Madam C. J. Walker proved that hard work, determination, and a great marketing strategy could make a business—and an industry—boom.

Madam C. J. Walker's "rags-to-riches" story has long inspired entrepreneurs, especially women and African Americans.

Daughter of Slaves

Madam C. J. Walker was born Sarah Breedlove on December 23, 1867, near Delta, Louisiana. Her parents, Owen and Minerva, were former slaves who still picked cotton on a plantation for very low wages. Sarah had a sister named Louvenia and four brothers. Sarah, however, was the first in her family to be born free after the Civil War ended.

The period after the Civil War in the South is called Reconstruction. Politics in the South were forced to change and there were many riots and attacks on African Americans. Sarah grew up in this environment of violence and **poverty**. Her mother died when she was around five years old. Her father remarried, but he also died not long after. She was now an orphan.

Although they were considered free after the war, many African Americans continued to work for their old owners for low pay.

Reconstruction

Reconstruction was the period after the American Civil War in the South. The North (the Union) won the war, and the South (the Confederacy) was left in ruin—physically and politically. Slavery was now illegal. The South's economy, which depended on slave labor, had fallen apart. Anger towards African Americans turned to great violence and **discrimination**, and many people were killed. Unfair laws were passed to enforce inequality between white people and black people, and African Americans suffered the effects of incomplete freedom.

Marrying Young

Sarah didn't have many options for advancement in her early life. She only had a formal education for about three months of her childhood. Violence, a bad cotton crop, and disease forced Sarah and her family from their home in Louisiana to Vicksburg, Mississippi. She had to live with her sister and her bad-tempered brother-in-law. It may be no surprise that she decided to run away. She was married at the age of only 14 to a man named Moses McWilliams.

In 1885, when Sarah was only 17 years old, she gave birth to her

Out of great tragedy, Sarah found her true passion in life—her daughter. Sarah worked tirelessly to provide for Lelia.

only child, Lelia. However, tragedy struck again when her husband died. Sarah was now both an orphan and a widow at only 20 years old.

New Life in St. Louis

Sarah was determined to do all she could to give her daughter a better life. In 1889, she moved to St. Louis, Missouri. At the time, St. Louis was a center of industry and trade. Sarah now lived close to all the luxuries of a big city, but she had to take a low-paying job as a washerwoman. She lived in a series of **tenements** in a poor, violent neighborhood. She also became trapped in an unhappy marriage to a man named John Davis.

Sarah also found opportunities in St. Louis. She joined St. Paul African Methodist Episcopal Church. There, she met and talked to important members of the community, such as doctors, teachers, and lawyers. She worked to pay for Lelia's education, and then, as an adult, Sarah went to night school to get her own education.

Sarah once recalled a day when she was washing clothes and thought to herself: "What are you going to do when you grow old and your back gets stiff? Who is going to take care of your little girl?"

A Solution to Her Problems

Sarah's hard life had a very physical consequence—she started losing her hair. It wasn't uncommon for poor African American women to have **scalp** irritation and diseases from poor **hygiene** and diet. Sarah set out to find a cure.

This led her to another entrepreneur named Annie Turnbo, who was later known as Annie Turnbo Malone. While there were some hair products at that time, few were suited to the texture of a black woman's hair. Turnbo sold her own product called "The Great Wonderful Hair Grower." It helped to straighten coarse, curled hair into smooth, long hair. She taught women a **regimen** of washing their hair, eating nutritious foods, and treating their hair with her special formula. Sarah tried the product and loved it. Soon, she was selling the product as one of Turnbo's many door-to-door agents.

Some say that Annie Turnbo Malone was actually the first female African American millionaire, though it can't be proven.

Annie Turnbo Malone

Annie Turnbo Malone was born in 1869. Like Sarah, she was the daughter of former slaves. By the time she was 20 years old, she'd created her own shampoo and scalp treatment that could straighten and grow hair. She sold her products door to door and in the streets. She moved to St. Louis, Missouri, and grew her business by hiring agents to sell her products. She was a leader in the African American community in St. Louis, where she opened a factory and beauty school.

Filling a Need

In 1905, Sarah moved to Denver, Colorado. She soon married a newspaper sales agent named Charles Joseph Walker. She decided to start her own business to sell hair products straight to African American women, much like Turnbo did. This was a mostly untapped industry, and she rose to fill the need.

Many African American women, like Sarah, had been told throughout their lives that their coarse, black hair wasn't beautiful. Also, many women didn't have access to regular baths and shampoo. They were left feeling unworthy and **self-conscious**.

Several companies sold hair products, but they used advertisements with before-and-after pictures of white women and suggested that white hair was the ideal. Sarah would use her business to create a new image of the beauty of straightened black hair.

Critics of Hair-Straightening

Hair straightening can be a very **controversial** issue in the African American community. Even today, many believe that black women should keep their hair natural. They see straightening hair as just another way that black women are pressured to look more "white." One famous critic of hair straightening was Booker T. Washington. He felt that hair-straightening products and skin-bleaching creams would continue the idea that white beauty was the only kind of beauty. This could lead to African Americans feeling inferior, or lesser than others.

The Walker System

Sarah renamed herself "Madam C. J. Walker." Her choice of name was important. It showed she had enough confidence to call herself "Madam." She didn't just sell a product—she sold a lifestyle.

With an initial investment of just $1.25, Walker created a product called "Madam Walker's Wonderful Hair Grower." It promised to leave hair smooth and help it grow. More importantly, it helped give many women confidence. Like Turnbo, Walker created a whole beauty system, one that included caring for one's scalp, applying lotions, and using hot iron combs.

This photo shows an original tin of Madam C. J. Walker's hair product.

For Long and Beautiful Hair!

Like That in the Portrats Above, Use

The Walker-Prosser Go.'s Wonderful Hair Grower

Manufactured by **C. J. Walker** and positively guaranteed to grow the hair from one-half to one inch per month or money refunded. A six week's trial treatment sent to any address, express prepaid for $1.50. Make money orders payable to

C. J. WALKER

1314 W. Chestnut St.,   **Louisville, Ky.**

Agents Wanted Everywhere. Write for Terms.

At first, Walker traveled around the country selling the product. It was also a mail-order business. Then, she hired agents to sell her product door to door. They received a **commission** for the products they sold, which gave them **incentive** to sell more.

Moving to Indianapolis

By 1910, Walker's business was booming. She decided to move its **headquarters** to Indianapolis, Indiana. At the company's peak, she had over 3,000 people working for her. Most of them were women.

Walker **incorporated** her business as the Madam C. J. Walker Manufacturing Company in 1910. She invested $10,000 in the corporation, and she made herself the main **shareholder** and director.

In Indianapolis, Walker built a factory and opened another school for her agents, whom she called "beauty culturalists." She set up similar affordable schools around the country. She once said, "I am not merely satisfied in making money for myself. I am endeavoring to provide employment for hundreds of women of my race." To further this goal, she established the National Negro Cosmetics Manufacturers Association in 1917.

The Madam C. J. Walker Manufacturing Company Indianapolis, 1911

Walker agents were empowered by their education and their opportunities for advancement. Walker believed so greatly in the potential of women that she made it a rule that only a woman could be the president of her company.

Amazing Marketing Skills

Walker's third husband was a skilled businessman in the newspaper world. He may have taught her marketing skills that greatly helped her business. Walker knew her audience was African American women like herself, so she went straight to them. She placed advertisements in many independent black newspapers. This got the word out about her product directly to the women reading the newspapers.

Walker also posted advertisements for her colleges. One of her brochures read: "Open your own shop; secure prosperity and freedom." The more agents she had, the greater her empire became. Even if women didn't see Walker's advertisements in the newspapers, they were sure to hear about her product by word of mouth from her many agents.

This 1920 advertisement talks about the "beauty" and "loveliness" Walker's products promised.

The Secret to Success

Sarah Breedlove's secret to creating the famous Madam C. J. Walker brand was simple: establish a personal connection. There were many cosmetics companies, but this company was owned by a black woman who made products for black women. Walker purposefully used her own face as the face of the company on the labels of the product. She also used her own portrait in the before-and-after shots instead of a white woman's portrait. It was her way of challenging the beauty standard of the time.

Walker was also selling a product that promised the secret to looking refined and, therefore, living a refined life. Walker's fleet of agents believed in the product's promise. These women were given the opportunity to run their own "businesses" and advance in life, and they were loyal to the company and eager to sell.

The Walker brand was special because it was a product for black women that was sold directly by black women. These women graduated from Walker's beauty school in 1939.

The Richest Woman Around

Walker's first goal was to provide for her daughter and send her to school. She did that, and much more. Walker was able to buy expensive homes and automobiles. She moved to New York City and bought a townhouse in Harlem, which she filled with the finest furniture and decorations.

Walker also built a country home in Irvington, New York, right on the Hudson River. One of her

Villa Lewaro

Unfortunately, Walker would only live in Villa Lewaro for a year before she died. It became a National Historic Landmark in 1976.

neighbors was John D. Rockefeller, one of America's wealthiest businessmen. A famous African American architect, Vertner Tandy, designed her country home. It was called Villa Lewaro. Important conferences between African American leaders were held at Walker's villa. It was a symbol of her wealth, and it showed just how far Walker had come as a woman and as an African American.

A Great Philanthropist

Madam C. J. Walker knew the injustices and poverty that African Americans faced. For that reason, when she made her money, she didn't keep it all to herself. She became a great philanthropist, which is a person who gives money to others for charity.

Walker gave back directly by educating and empowering her agents. This lifted many African American women out of poverty and gave them business opportunities they wouldn't normally have had. Walker also offered employee bonuses and prizes to agents who performed works of charity.

Walker gave money to many major African American organizations, such as the National Association for the Advancement of Colored People (NAACP). She also gave to the National Association of Colored Women and many other charities that benefited the African American community.

Walker showed pride in her heritage by giving back to the African American community.

NAACP

The National Association for the Advancement of Colored People (NAACP) was founded on February 12, 1909. It grew into the country's largest civil rights organization. It was formed in response to the violence inflicted on African Americans during the early 1900s. The goal of the organization is to rid the country of racial discrimination. The NAACP played a large part in securing many civil rights during the American civil rights movement in the 1950s and 1960s and continues to fight for equality today.

The Madam's Legacy

Walker's beauty empire greatly impacted the hair products industry in the 20th century. Many African American women today use hair-straightening products, such as chemical straighteners called relaxers and hot combs, which are now mostly electric. Other women prefer keeping their hair natural to celebrate their cultural heritage.

Madam C. J. Walker spent much of her life in poverty. However, over the course of her life, she built a beauty empire and gained great wealth as an entrepreneur. Unfortunately, she died at the age of 51 in her beautiful new home, Villa Lewaro. Walker's legacy lived on through her daughter, Lelia, who became a well-known figure in the Harlem Renaissance. Her legacy also lives on in the lives of the women she empowered and the women who are still inspired by her today.

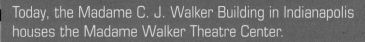

Today, the Madame C. J. Walker Building in Indianapolis houses the Madame Walker Theatre Center.

Lelia Walker

Lelia Walker was born in 1885, the only child of Madam C. J. Walker. She later changed her name to A'Lelia. She oversaw Lelia College and managed the Pittsburgh branch of her mother's company. After her mother's death, Lelia became president of the company. In 1927, Lelia turned part of her mother's Harlem townhouse into a salon called the Dark Tower, which hosted many Harlem Renaissance writers and artists, such as Langston Hughes and Zora Neale Hurston. She was known for throwing many grand parties. Lelia died in 1931 at only 46 years old.

A Timeline of Madam C. J. Walker's Life

1867 — Sarah Breedlove is born near Delta, Louisiana.

1872 — Sarah's mother dies.

1874 — Sarah's father dies.

1882 — Sarah marries Moses McWilliams at the age of 14.

1885 — Sarah gives birth to a daughter, Lelia.

1887 — Sarah's first husband dies. She is a widow at 20.

1894 — Sarah marries her second husband, John Davis. They divorce in 1903.

1905 — Sarah moves to Denver, Colorado. She sells hair products for Annie Turnbo, but also starts making her own products.

1906 — Sarah and her third husband travel to southern and eastern states to spread the word about her product.

1908 — Sarah establishes Lelia College, a school for her agents, in Pittsburgh, Pennsylvania.

1910 — Sarah moves her headquarters to Indianapolis, Indiana. Sarah incorporates her company with herself as the main shareholder. It's now called the Madam C. J. Walker Manufacturing Company.

1912 — Sarah divorces C. J. Walker but keeps his name.

1919 — Sarah dies at Villa Lewaro.